A Life of Glory

A Life of Glory

A Selection of Poems by
George Herbert
for
Reflection

Edited and introduced by
Marianne Dorman

The Pentland Press Limited
Edinburgh Cambridge Durham

First published in 1992 by
The Pentland Press Ltd.
5 Hutton Close
South Church
Bishop Auckland
Durham

ISBN 1 872795 78 1

Set in 10 point Times by Print Origination (NW)
Limited, Formby, Liverpool, L37 8EG.
Printed and bound by Antony Rowe
Limited, Chippenham, Wiltshire, SN14 6LH.

Thy life is God's, thy time is gone,
And is His right.
He is Thy night at noon: He is at night
Thy noon alone.
The crop is His, for He hath sown

Herbert, Vol. 2, p. 163

To the Glory of God

AND IN THANKSGIVING FOR THE LIFE OF CHRIST
IN
GEORGE HERBERT
AND
IN
NEVILLE JAMES ELEY
MY PARISH PRIEST
1967–1975

Acknowledgement

I am very grateful to a young artist, Mr. Chris Maple, who lives in Salisbury, not far from George Herbert's parish church of St. Andrew's, Bemerton, for the sketches of this church for the front cover.

Table of Contents

Foreword

The poetry of George Herbert is one of the greatest treasures of the Church of England. Into his lines Herbert put the whole story of his relationship with God. It was a love relationship, certainly, but it was also a relationship of struggle. Through conflict he came to know peace, through darkness and at times despair he came to know a deep and serene confidence in God's mercy.

In this book Marianne Dorman has aimed to introduce Herbert to us in such a way as to make his work more easily accessible to readers today. At first sight Herbert's poems can seem difficult. The style and the way of thought is not our own and they do not yield their full meaning to one quick reading. These are poems which have come from much prayer and meditation and they demand prayer and meditation and also time on our part if we are to appreciate them at their true value. To those who are prepared to stay with them they will prove endlessly rewarding. There are few poets whose work improves so much with constant rereading. Coming back, perhaps after years, to a poem you thought you knew well you will suddenly find new meaning and light shining out from it. These are poems which were written with much love as well as with deep thought. It is love which speaks to us through these pages, God's love which may surprise us by drawing out our love in response.

Canon A. M. Allchin
Director of The St. Theosovia Centre, Oxford.

Preface

*Wherein his faithful discharge was such, as may
make him justly a companion to the primitive Saints
and a pattern or more for the age he lived in.*[1]

Invariably when I think of George Herbert, I immediately recall the most
spiritual and beautiful of all his poems, *Love bade me welcome*,
beckoning us to the delights of heavenly Bread, and those poems, such as
Teach me my God and King and *King of glory, King of peace*, which I
have sung as hymns all my life. They embrace the crux of the Gospel:
Love given for sinful man, and continually given in the Blessed
Sacrament, and man in turn, responding to Love in his unworthy way, 'I
will love Thee,' with 'the cream of all my heart'. They also contain the
Christian concepts of service and devotion, praise and thanksgiving,
'Seven whole days, not one in seven, I will praise Thee'. Such poems
have inspired not only me, but many others, to live in joy and praise:
'with my utmost art/I will sing Thee,' and be transformed by Love.
Simone Weil once declared that by concentrating completely on reciting
Love bade me welcome, she was able to rise above the physical
oppressive affliction of a migraine, and be bathed in Love.

This book is designed for those who wish to know in a simple
presentation something about the life and character of George Herbert,
priest and poet, and to draw closer to God in their everyday living of the
Christian life, by meditating on some of his poems. These have been
suitably arranged under three headings: worship, the Christian year and
Christian character for easy access and meditation.

To make reading easier, I have slightly modified spelling, other than
when it interferes with rhythm, rhyme or poetic effects such as assonance
and alliteration. The changes are very minor. For example *only* for
onely; *thankful* for *thankfull*; *join* for *joyn*; and *wrestling* for *wrastling*.

Oxford
The Commemoration of George Herbert: Priest, Pastor, Poet.
27th February 1992.

The Life of George Herbert

George Herbert was one of the most lovable members the *Ecclesia Angli-cana* has ever had. Lovable because his life was living in Christ:

> *Thou art my loveliness, my life, my light,*
> *Beauty alone to me:*
> *Thy bloody death, and undeserved, makes thee*
> *Pure red and white.*[2]

Lovable because it was shrouded in humility, as expressed in his motto, *Less than the least of God's mercies'*,[3] with which he concluded all things.

Lovable because of its complete consecration to Christ:

> *Christ is my only head,*
> *My alone only heart and breast,*
> *My only music, striking me e'en dead;*
> *That to the old man I may rest,*
> *And be in him new drest.*[4]

Lovable because through the grief he suffered in times of spiritual blackness, it became times of perseverance and faithfulness:

> *Where is my God? what hidden place*
>   *Conceals Thee still?*
> *What covert dare eclipse thy face?*
>   *Is it thy will?*

...

> *Since then my grief must be as large*
> *As is Thy space,*
> *Thy distance from me; see my charge,*
> *Lord, see my case.*[5]

The Priest

> *But the holy men of God such vessels are,*
> *As serve him up, who all the world commands.*[6]

The whole tone of this holy man's life was priestly, no better illustrated than in the opening sentence of his work, *A Priest to The Temple*. He 'is exceeding exact in his life, being holy, just, prudent, temperate, bold, grave in all his ways.'[7] In his rather short life (1593–1633), Herbert spent but two and a half years as a priest, and so he did not have much time to practise what he preached in *A Country Parson*, but in the spirit of St. Peter's meaning of the 'royal priesthood', he was truly priestly for most of his life. Undoubtedly his preparation for his priestly ministry and indeed his Christ-like living was built on the spiritual foundation which he received from his remarkable mother. From her he had learnt that a depth to the spiritual life was grounded in learning to still the soul and to live each moment with God. Every day was special, and offered to Him:

> *I cannot ope' mine eyes,*
> *But Thou art ready there to catch*
> *My morning-soul and sacrifice:*
> *Then we must needs for that day make a match.*[8]

and at the end of the day the searching for how it was spent:

> *What have I brought Thee home*
> *For this thy love? have I discharged the debt?*
> *Which this days favour did beget?*
> *I ran; but all I brought, was foam.*[9]

Despite the shortcomings of the day, Herbert knew he could rest in the assurance of God's ever abiding love:

> *My God, Thou art all love.*
> *Not one poor minute 'scapes thy breast,*
> *But brings a favour from above;*
> *And in this love, more than in bed, I rest.*[10]

From living out the faith at Cambridge, beginning as an undergraduate and through to being Public Orator, he experienced the very substance of it through prayer, the consciousness of sin and his own unworthiness, the meaning of repentance and confession, and the hope of eternal glory through Christ's redeeming acts. His struggle and perseverance in living the Christian life are reflected in his poems. In fact most of his poems are prayers. Thus from his own experiences towards growing in holiness and witnessing for Christ in Cambridge, he was able to write his exhortation on how he felt a priest should exercise his ministry and live out his personal life. For the latter it was also important that the parson's life be always exemplary in which he 'girds up his loins' and 'puts on the whole armour of God' and 'keeps his watch and ward, night and day, against the proper and peculiar temptations of his state of life, which are principally these two, spiritual pride and impurity of heart'. Thus the purpose of his life was to 'to put on the profound humility and the exact temperance of Our Lord Jesus.'[11]

According to *A Country Parson* the most important duties for the parson were to pray, take Divine Service and administer the sacrament, both with and on behalf of his people.[12] In preparation for these the parson composed 'himself to all possible reverence; [lifted] up his heart and hands, and eyes, and [used] all other gestures which may express a hearty and unfeigned devotion.' He achieved this by:

> *being truly touched and amazed with the majesty of God, before whom he presents himself; yet not as himself alone, but as presenting with himself the whole congregation; whose sins he then bears and brings with his own to the heavenly Altar to be bathed and washed in the sacred Laver of Christ's blood.*[13]

On Sunday, 'O day most calm, most bright,' that very special day of the week, when 'my Saviour rose', and when 'heavens gate stands open',[14] Herbert believed that an extra careful preparation was needed. Thus on awakening he saw the priest 'as a market-man is when the market-day comes.' Hence:

> *Besides his ordinary prayers, he makes a peculiar one for a blessing on the exercises of the day. That nothing befall him unworthy of that*

Majesty, before which he is to present himself, but that all may be done with reverence to His glory, and with edification to His flock, humbly beseeching his Master, that how or whenever He punish him, it be not in his ministry.

His next concern was for his people; and thus he prayed:

That the Lord would be pleased to sanctify them all, that they may come with holy hearts and awful minds into the congregation, and that the good God would pardon all those who come with less prepared hearts than they ought.[15]

Once one has visited his tiny church of St. Andrew's, Bemerton, about a mile's walk from Salisbury cathedral via the old mill, one can envisage Herbert being the kind of priest he writes about in his very small parish. Of course there is no surviving written evidence of his time as the incumbent of St. Andrew's for us to know whether he actually did fulfil all the high standards he had set out in his book. Given the prayerfulness of his poetry, I think he probably did.

His Induction

But Thou art fire, sacred and hallow'd fire;
And I but earth and clay: should I presume
To wear thy habit, the severe attire
My slender compositions might consume.
I am both foul and brittle much unfit
*   To deal in holy Writ.*[16]

Herbert's main pastoral ministry was exercised in the parish of St. Andrew's, Bemerton and Fuggleston, St. Peter's, about a mile from Salisbury Cathedral to which he walked twice a week for Evensong, where 'his time spent in prayer and Cathedral music elevated his soul, and was his heaven upon earth,'[17] His induction to the cure of all souls took place about five months before he was ordained priest by Bishop Davenant on the 19th September 1630. Although only a deacon his dedication is no less, as revealed in his prostration 'on the ground before the altar' as he rededicated his life to God just before his induction,[18] and illustrated in this letter to his good friend Woodnot, written also just prior to his induction, in which he declared:

But in God and His service is a fullness of all joy and pleasure, and no satiety. And I will now use all my endeavours to bring my relations and dependants to a love and reliance on Him who never fails those who trust Him. But, above all, I will be sure to live well, because the virtuous life of a clergyman is the most powerful eloquence to persuade all that see it to reverence and love, and at least to desire to live like him.

Herbert explained why this exemplary living was so essential:

And this I will do, because I know we live in an age that has more need of good example than precepts. And I beseech that God, who has honoured me so much as to call me to serve Him at His altar, that as by His special grace He has put into my heart these good desires and resolutions; so He will, by His assisting grace, give me ghostly strength to bring the same to good effect. And I beseech Him, that my humble and charitable life may so win upon others, as to bring glory to my JESUS, whom I have this day taken to be my Master and Governor: and I am so proud of His service that I will always observe and obey and do His will and always call him Jesus my Master, and I will always condemn my birth, or any title or dignity that can be conferred upon me, when I shall compare them with my title of being a priest and serving at the altar of Jesus my Master.[19]

The Pastor

Lord, I have invited all,
And I shall
Still invite, still call to Thee:
For it seems but just and right
In my sight,
Where is all, there all should be.[20]

The pastor, and one assumes that includes George Herbert, was 'a father to his flock'. Apart from the basic courteousness to his parishioners, he spent his afternoons visiting his people, where 'first he blesses' their home, 'and then as he finds the persons of the house employed, so he forms his discourse.' He comforted the 'sick or afflicted with loss of friend . . . or any ways distressed', and performed many acts of charity to the poor.[21] Indeed he used to say that 'when he arises in the morning,' he always thought of 'what good deeds he can do that day, and presently does them.' If a day transpired without his exercising 'his charity', he counted 'that day lost.'[22] Walton gave various accounts of how Herbert practised this, often when out walking. He cites for instance when Herbert on his way to Salisbury met the 'poor man with a poorer horse which had fallen under [its] load', and how Herbert had stopped and helped to reload, thus arriving at Salisbury Cathedral for Evensong a little dishevelled![23]

Part of the work of a country parson involved his caring for the church and encouraging his people to do likewise, so that 'all things be decent'.

> *Avoid, profaneness; come not here:*
> *Nothing but holy, pure, and clear,*
> *Or that which groaneth to be so,*
> *May at his peril further go.*[24]

Herbert recognized that it was useless teaching the people to behave decently and reverently during worship while ever the church was dilapidated and in need of repair.[25] This meant having 'walls plastered, windows glazed, floors paved, seats whole, firm and uniform.' It also meant 'that the pulpit, and desk and Communion table and font be as they ought, for those great duties that are performed in them.' Cleanliness was also necessary, and so the 'church [must] be swept, and kept clean without dust, or cobwebs, and at great festivals strawed and stuck with boughs, and perfumed with incense'. Moreover 'all the books appointed by authority [should] be there... not torn, or fouled, but whole and clean, and well bound.' The Communion cloth too must be 'fitting and sightly' and made 'of fine linen or cloth and all kept sweet and clean in a strong and decent chest with a chalice with a handsome and seemly carpet of good and costly stuff. There must also be a chalice and cover, and a stoop or flagon; and a basin for alms, and offerings.'[26]

His Teaching

> *The shepherds sing; and shall I silent be?*
> *My God, no hymn for Thee?*
> *My soul's a shepherd too; a flock it feeds*
> *Of thoughts, and words and deeds.*
> *Thy pasture is Thy word; the streams, Thy grace*
> *Enriching all the place.*[27]

'Edification to [the] flock' was vital, for not only must he, the parson, be
pious, but also his people. Hence he must instruct his people in sermon
and catechism. Among the matters he had to teach them was 'how to
carry themselves in Divine Service', with 'all possible reverence', so that
there was not any 'talking, or sleeping, or gazing, or leaning, or half-
kneeling, or any undutiful behaviour.'[28]

> *When once thy foot enters the church, be bare.*
> *God is more there, than thou: for thou art there*
> *Only by His permission. Then beware,*
> *And make thyself all reverence and fear.*
> *Kneeling ne'er spoil'd silk stocking: quit thy state.*
> *All equal are within the church's gate.*[29]

Furthermore 'when they sit or stand or kneel' all must be done in a
straight, and steady posture, as attending to what is done in the Church.'
During the actual service 'everyone, man and child,' were to answer
'aloud both *Amen* and all other answers which are in the clerk's and
people's part to answer.'[30] Posture and participation, Herbert knew,
would contribute significantly to concentration:

> *Let vain or busy thoughts have there no part:*
> *Bring not thy plough, thy plots, thy pleasures thither.*
> *Christ purged His temple; so must thou thy heart.*
> *All worldly thoughts are but thieves met together*
> *To cozen thee. Look to thy actions well:*
> *For churches are either our heaven or hell.*

Therefore:

> *In time of service seal up both thine eyes,*
> *And send them to thine heart; that, spying sin,*
> *They may weep out the stains by them did rise:*
> *Those doors being shut, all by the ear comes in,*
> *Who marks in church-time others' symmetry,*
> *Makes all their beauty his deformity.*[31]

The receiving of the Blessed Sacrament had to be approached with great
reverence and humility; 'he who comes to the Sacrament has the
confidence of a guest, and he who kneels confesses himself an unworthy
one, and therefore differs from other feasters...' Herbert admonished
the feaster 'who sits or lies out up to an Apostle: Contentiousness in a

feast of charity is more scandal than any posture.'[32]

Herbert realized that once parishioners knew how to conduct themselves in church, they could then be more attentive to sermons. Much care was needed in preparing and delivering sermons so as to guide the flock along the path of holiness. These sermons, never exceeding an hour, 'were constantly taken out of the Gospel for the day', in which the pastor always explained 'why the Church did appoint that portion of scripture to be that day read'. Moreover he showed how the various collects related 'to the Gospel or the Epistle'. He also taught them the meaning not only of the collects, but also the other prayers and responses in the Church services, so that his people would know 'that the whole service of the Church was a reasonable, and therefore an acceptable sacrifice to God'. He also 'made them to understand how happy they be who are freed from the incumbrance of that law which our forefathers groaned under; namely from the legal sacrifices, and from the many ceremonies of the Levitical law'. Instead they have 'so many and so great blessings, by being born since the days of our Saviour'. Therefore Herbert maintained, 'it must be an acceptable sacrifice to Almighty God for them to acknowledge those blessings daily, and stand up and worship and say as Zacharias did, *Blessed be the Lord God of Israel for he has visited and redeemed his people* . . .'. As a result they now live 'to see and enjoy the benefit of it, in His birth, in His life, His passion, His resurrection, and ascension into heaven, where He now sits sensible of our temptations and infirmities; and where He now is at present time making intercession for us to His and our father.'[33]

Another reason for taking so much preparation over sermons was because they were also a means to prayer:

> *Resort to sermons, but to prayers most:*
> *Praying's the end of preaching. O be drest;*
> *Stay not for the other pin: why, thou hast lost*
> *A joy for its worth worlds. Thus hell doth jest*
> *Away thy blessings, and extremely flout thee,*
> *Thy clothes being fast, but thy soul loose about thee.*[34]

Ideally this meant that parishioners received instruction on the importance of prayer.

> *Of what an easy quick access,*
> *My blessed Lord, art Thou! how suddenly*
> *May our requests thine ear invade!*[35]

Herbert advocated that it was necessary that all Christians should pray
fervently; 'twice a day, every day of the week and four times on Sunday,
if they be well.' That was the minimum; any less meant that a Christian
'cannot...maintain himself in a Christian state'. Hence congregations
were encouraged to follow the example of the many godly persons who
'have added some hours of prayer, as at nine, or at three, or at midnight,
or as they think fit.'[36]

Herbert also emphasised the importance for *quiet prayer*; the need 'to
be alone', in order to grow spiritually.

> *Salute thy self: see what thy soul does wear.*
> *Dare to look in thy chest, for 'tis thine own:*
> *And tumble up and down what thou find'st there.*[37]

Once alone the starting point for devotions was the confession of sins;
until we have confessed our *wretchedness*, 'we are not capable of that
mercy which we acknowledge we need, and pray for; but having, in the
prayer of our Lord, begged pardon for those sins which we
have...confessed'; we are then able 'to praise Him'.[38]

Above all he taught the meaning and practice of love in the Christian
life.

> *Come, my Joy, my Love, my Heart:*
> *Such a Joy, as none can move:*
> *Such a Love, as none can part:*
> *Such a Heart, as joys in love.*[39]

Wherever there is love, there is God, for He is Love. This is made so
abundantly clear in probably the loveliest of all Herbert's poems, *Love
bade me welcome*, in which he concludes:

> *You must sit down, says Love, and taste my meat:*
> *So I did sit and eat.*[40]

Such Love is the consummation of the Christian life, and it is this Love
which Herbert stressed must be given and extended to all after the
dismissal from the Eucharist. Especially important therefore was
'mutual love', evident when prayers are 'offered for each other,' and
when 'the holy angels look down from heaven, and are ready to carry
such charitable desires to God Almighty, and He as ready to receive

them.' Herbert likened a Christian congregation which prayed 'with one heart and one voice, in one reverent and humble posture' to 'Jerusalem that is peace with itself'.[41]

Sunday afternoons was the time the pastor catechized the young and the old, in order 'to infuse a competent knowledge of salvation in every one of his flock' so as 'to multiply and build up this knowledge to a spiritual temple'. This then was to be put 'into practice' to reform their lives.[42]

His Parishioners

> *Restore to God his due in tithe and time:*
> *... Sundays observe: ...*
> *Twice on the day His due is understood;*
> *For all the week thy food so oft He gave thee.*[43]

Herbert probably had no more than a couple of dozen or so souls living in the bounds of his parish. Perhaps it was possible for most of these to pray daily with him in the little church of St. Andrew's. Walton in his biography of Herbert revealed that 'most of his parishioners and many gentlemen in the neighbourhood' often formed part of the daily congregation. Indeed 'some of the meaner sort of his parish did so love and reverence Mr. Herbert that they would let their plough rest when Mr. Herbert's saint's bell rung to prayers, that they might also offer their devotion to God with him; and would then return ... to their plough.'[44] One would like to think that his parishioners could say, like Herbert:

> *Christ is my only head,*
> *My alone only heart and breast,*
> *My only music.*[45]

His Devotion to the English Church

Herbert had a profound love for the English Church, his spiritual Mother on earth, so aptly expressed in his poem *The British Church*:

I joy, dear Mother, when I view
Thy perfect lineaments and hue
            Both sweet and bright:
Beauty in thee takes up her place,
And dates her letters from thy face,
            When she does write.

A fine aspect in fit array,
Neither too mean, nor yet too gay,
            Shows who is best.
Outlandish looks may not compare;
For all they either painted are,
            Or else undrest.

She on the hills, which wantonly
Allures all in hope to be
            By her preferr'd,
Hath kiss'd so long her painted shrines,
That e'en her face by kissing shines,
            For her reward.

She in the valley is so shy
Of dressing, that her hair doth lie
            About her ears:
While she avoids her neighbours pride,
She wholly goes on th' other side,
            And nothing wears.

But, dearest Mother, (what those miss)
The mean, thy praise and glory is,
            And long may be.
Blessed be God, whose love it was
To double-moat Thee with His grace,
            And none but Thee.[46]

His Love of Music

Sweetest of sweet, I thank you: when displeasure
Did through my body wound my mind,
You took me thence, and in your house of pleasure
A dainty lodging me assign'd.[47]

Herbert himself was an accomplished musician. Thus it is no wonder that
he could say 'his chiefest recreation was music, in which heavenly art he

was a most excellent master.' Many of his poems 'he set and sung to his lute and viol'.

Walton tells us 'his love to music was such that he went usually twice every week, on certain appointed days to the cathedral church in Salisbury; and at his return would say, that his time spent in prayer and Cathedral music elevated his soul, and was his heaven on earth.'[48] For Herbert music was 'the way to heaven's door', and without it life was comfortless:

> *Comfort, I'll die; for if you post from me,*
> *Sure I shall do so, and much more:*
> *But if I travel in your company,*
> *You know the way to heaven's door.*[49]

His Love of Nature

> *Hark, how the birds do sing,*
> *And woods do ring,*
> *All creatures have their joys.*[50]

Did Herbert's awareness of the world of nature extend out of his pleasure of walking or was his joy from walking derived from his love and appreciation of nature? Probably these two pleasures simply mingled. When at Bemerton Herbert loved to walk across the fields and to roam the countryside. It was a time of reflecting upon God's beauty in creation and praising Him for such loveliness. So many intimate details are sketched, that one can imagine Herbert hovering over the pigeons as they fed their offspring, or being mesmerized by the beauty of a rose. Every flower, every tree, every plant; the wheat blades, even the luscious weeds, as well as the birds, butterflies and bees; all had their unique attractiveness, as each was created specially by God, and therefore were to be reverenced:

> *Bees work for man; and yet they never bruise*
> *Their master's flower, but leave it, having done,*
> *As fair as ever, and as fit to use;*
> *So both the flower doth stay, and honey run.*

Sheep eat the grass, and dung the ground for more:
Trees after bearing drop their leaves for soil:
Springs vent their streams, and by exposure get
store:
Clouds cool by heat, and baths by cooling boil.

Who hath the virtue to express the rare
And curious virtues of both herbs and stones?
Is there an herb for that? O that thy care.
Would show a root, that gives expressions!

...

How harsh are thorns to pears! and yet they make
A better hedge, and need less reparation.

...

Thy creatures leap not, but express a feast,
Where all the guests sit close and nothing wants.
Frogs marry fish and flesh; bats; bird and beast;
Sponges, non-sense and sense; mines, the earth and
plants.[51]

The Poet

There was in it the picture of a divine soul in every page; and that the whole
book was such a harmony of holy passions as would enrich the world with
pleasure and piety.[52]

So wrote Ferrar after reading the collection of poems Herbert had sent to
him on his death-bed to do as he felt fit.[53]

Herbert began to write his poetry seriously while at Trinity College,
Cambridge. The first poems published in 1612 were two memorial poems
in Latin for Prince Henry. The collection of sacred poems and pious
ejaculations, making up *The Temple* paint his own struggles: 'pluck out
thy dart, and heal my troubled breast', towards perfection, or are 'a
picture of the many spiritual conflicts that have passed between God and
my soul, before I would subject mine to the will of Jesus, my Master, in
whose service I have now found perfect freedom'.[54] His poems also
oozed with the abundant goodness of God, exacting from him deep-
rooted praise:

Lord, I will [sing] *and speak thy praise,*
Thy praise alone.

My busy heart shall spin it all my days:
And when it stops for want of store,
Then will I wring it with a sigh or groan,
That Thou mayst yet have more.[55]

Like his contemporary, Lancelot Andrewes, so much of his teaching was given through nature imagery. For instance in this stanza, Herbert compares spiritual renewal after a period of deadness like this:

Who would have thought my shrivel'd heart
Could have recover'd greenness? It was gone
Quite under ground; as flowers depart
To see their Mother-root, when they have blown;
Where they together
All the hard weather,
Dead to the world, keep house unknown.[56]

Herbert's approach to writing his poetry was mainly allegorical. In order to teach some spiritual concept he would focus on something abstract. For instance the imprisonment of sin and its ultimate release was taught by focusing on the 'church – lock and key'.[57] Indeed, most of Herbert's teaching is through the extended metaphor.

Herbert's Mother

Much has been written about George Herbert's piety, yet his mother as Lady Danvers, after her second marriage, through her own holiness in living must have inspired her son many times to lead a life of saintliness. At her death, her close friend, John Donne delivered the funeral oration. It is from this that we glean so much of her piety. Donne tells us that 'the rule of all her civil actions was religious, [and] . . . the rule of her religion was the Scripture; [while] her rule for her . . . understanding of the Scripture was the Church.' In this and all her religious observances she was a faithful member of the English Church, never diverting 'towards the Papist in undervaluing the Scripture; nor towards the Separatists in undervaluing the Church' – that church in which she was baptized, 'brought up her children', attended with her family the services according to the Prayer Book not only on Sundays, but as 'often as these [church's] doors were opened.'[58]

In her home on Sunday evenings, and with the whole family, her 'last act' of the day ended on a cheerful note with the 'singing of psalms'.[59] She was very generous in her charity, especially towards the poor labourers, and after them, to the 'idle and vagrant beggars'. Thus her home was also an 'almshouse for the poor, [and] a hospital for ministering relief to the sick'. Donne added, 'And truly, the love of doing good in this kind of ministering to the sick was the honey that was spread over all her bread; the air, the perfume, that breathed over all her house.' She was 'eyes to the blind, and hands and feet to the lame.' The only blight on her soul was an 'occasional melancholy' in declining years in times of sickness, yet even this 'never eclipsed, never interrupted her cheerful confidence and assurance in God'. When her last hours came, 'she showed no fear'; in prayers of the church she still answered clearly the congregational responses, almost to the last moment. When this came she died 'without any struggling, any disorder; but her death-bed was as quiet as her grave.'[60]

His Friendship with Nicholas Ferrar

Thy friend put in thy bosom: wear his eyes
Still in thy heart, that he may see what's there.
If cause require, thou art his sacrifice;
Thy drops of blood must pay down all his fear.[61]

Both Herbert and Ferrar had been contemporaries at Cambridge, after which their friendship was maintained 'by loving and endearing letters'. Both had short lives in which they lived out to the full the Christian faith, the strength for which came from the hours spent in prayer, meditation, stillness, self-discipline and a complete dedication of their beings to God. No wonder Herbert always referred to Ferrar as his 'most entire friend and brother' as they were bonded in their deep spiritual awareness and piety. Nicholas, apart from his family for whom they were written, shared his writings only with Herbert, and when the latter knew he was dying he entreated his friend Mr. Duncan to 'deliver this little book to my dear brother Ferrar, and tell him he will find in it a picture of the many spiritual conflicts that have passed between God and my soul before I could subject mine to the will of Jesus my master in whose service I have now found perfect freedom.' He desired Nicholas 'to read it', and if he thought 'it may turn to the advantage of any... dejected poor soul, let it be made public, if not let him burn it, for I and it are less than the least of God's mercies.'

He also entreated his brother 'to continue daily prayers for me', and directed Mr. Duncan to 'tell him my heart is fixed on that place where true joy is only to be found; and that I long to be there and do wait for my appointed change with hope and patience.'[62]

Before his induction at Bemerton, Herbert had been the prebend of Layton in the diocese of Lincoln, close to Little Gidding. As the parish church was in a decaying state the Ferrar family helped Herbert to repair and beautify it. Herbert expressed his gratitude in the following letter:

> *My dear Brother, I thank you heartily for Layton, your care, your counsel, your cost. And as I am glad for the thing, so no less glad for the heart, that God has given you and yours to pious works.*[63]

Nicholas survived his dear friend by approximately four and a half years. He died on the 4th December 1637.

Death

> *'I have practised mortification, and endeavoured to die daily that I might not die eternally... I must die or not come to that happy place. And this is my content, that I am going daily towards it.'*[64]

During his lifetime Herbert had cherished all that was beautiful, good and noble. As he approached death he realized even these had to be let go. 'I now look back upon the pleasures of my life past, and see the content I have taken in beauty, in wit, in music, and pleasant conversation are now all past by me like a dream, or as a shadow that returns not, and are now all become dead to me or I to them.'

As death approached he overcame the last assault on his soul 'by the merits of his master Jesus.' The physical agony in this conquest had so distressed the women who watched by him that they were overcome with great grief. Such was the weeping of his wife and three nieces, Herbert asked them to withdraw to the next room, otherwise their dolorous countenance 'could make his death uncomfortable'.

Shortly afterwards, once his affairs had been settled with dear Mr. Woodnot, Herbert knew he was now all prepared for death: 'I am now ready to die,' and prayed, 'Lord, forsake me not, now my strength fails me; but grant me mercy for the merits of my Jesus. And now Lord – Lord now receive my soul.'

As he had lived, so 'he died, like a saint unspotted of the world, full of alms deeds, full of humility, and all the example of a virtuous life.'[65]

Summary of Herbert's Life

3/4/1593	his birth – fifth son of Richard and Magdalen Herbert.[66]
1605	sent to Westminster School under the care of Dr. Neile.
1608	elected to Trinity College, Cambridge.
1609	began his B.A. and vowed his life's dedication to the writing of sacred poetry.
1612	received his B.A. degree.
3/10/1614	elected a minor Fellow of Trinity College.
15/3/1615–6	elected a major Fellow of Trinity College.
1616	received M.A.
10/6/1618	appointed Praelector (or reader) in Rhetoric.
21/1/1619–20	elected Orator.
1625 or 26	ordained Deacon.
5/7/1626	installed as Prebend of Layton ecclesia, and shortly with the encouragement and support of the Ferrars began the rebuilding and the beautifying of the parish church.
5/3/1628–9	married Jane Danvers in the parish church of Edington.
26/4/1630	inducted to the parishes of St. Andrew's, Bemerton and Fuggleston St. Peter.
19/9/1630	ordained priest in Salisbury Cathedral by Bishop Davenant.
1/3/1632–3	his death.

Worship

Praise

How should I praise Thee, Lord! how should my rhymes
Gladly engrave thy love in steel,
If what my soul doth feel sometimes,
   My soul might ever feel!

Although there were some forty heavens, or more,
   Sometimes I peer above them all;
   Sometimes I hardly reach a score,
     Sometimes to hell I fall.[67]

Cho. Let all the world in every corner sing,
          My God and King.

   Vers. The heavens are not too high,
       His praise may thither fly;
       The earth is not too low,
       His praises there may grow.

Cho. Let all the world in every corner sing,
          My God and King.

Vers. The church with psalms must shout,
    No door can keep them out:
    But above all, the heart
    Must bear the longest part.

Cho. Let all the world in every corner sing,
               My God and King.[68]

King of glory, King of peace,
    I will love Thee:
And that love may never cease,
    I will move Thee.

Thou hast granted my request,
    Thou hast heard me:
Thou didst note my working breast,
    Thou hast spared me.

Wherefore with my utmost art
    I will sing Thee,
And the cream of all my heart
    I will bring Thee.

Though my sins against me cried,
    Thou didst clear me;
And alone, when they replied,
    Thou didst hear me.

Seven whole days, not one in seven,
    I will praise Thee.
In my heart, though not in heaven,
    I can raise Thee.

Thou grew'st soft and moist with tears,
    Thou relentedst.
And when Justice call'd for fears,
    Thou dissentedst.

Small it is, in this poor sort
    To enrol Thee:
Ee'n eternity is too short
    To extol Thee.[69]

Preparation for Public Worship

I go to Church; help me to wings, and I
    Will thither fly;
  Or, if I mount unto the sky,
      I will do more.

...

O raise me then! Poor bees, that work all day,
    Sting my delay,
  Who have a work, as well as they,
      And much, much more.[70]

Sundays observe: think when the bells do chime,
'Tis angels music; therefore come not late.
  God then deals blessings: If a king did so,
  Who would not haste, nay give, to see the show?

Twice on the day His due is understood;
For all the week thy food so oft He gave thee.
Thy cheer is mended; bate not of the food,
Because 'tis better, and perhaps may save thee.
  Thwart not the Almighty God: O be not cross.
  Fast when thou wilt but then, 'tis gain not loss.

Though private prayer be a brave design,
Yet public hath more promises, more love:
And love's a weight to hearts, to eyes a sign.
We all are but cold suitors; let us move
  Where it is warmest. Leave thy six and seven;
  Pray with the most: for where most pray, is heaven.

In time of service seal up both thine eyes,
And send them to thine heart; that spying sin,
They may weep out the stains by them did rise:
Those doors being shut, all by the ear comes in.
  Who marks in church-time others' symmetry,
  Makes all their beauty his deformity.[71]

Come, bring thy gift. If blessings were as slow
As men's returns, what would become of fools?
What hast thou there? a heart? but is it pure?
Search well and see; for hearts have many holes.
Yet one pure heart is nothing to bestow.
In Christ two natures met to be thy cure.[72]

Meditative Prayer

A kind of tune, which all things hear and fear;

Softness, and peace, and joy, and love, and bliss,
    Exalted Manna, gladness of the best,
    Heaven in ordinary, man well drest,
The milky way, the bird of Paradise,

    Church-bells beyond the stars heard, the soul's blood,
    The land of spices; something understood.[73]

* * *

When my devotions could not pierce,
    Thy silent ears;
Then was my heart broken, as was my verse;
    My breast was full of fears
    And disorder:

My bent thoughts, like a brittle bow,
    Did fly asunder:
Each took his way; some would to pleasures go,
    Some to the wars and thunder
    Of alarms.

...

Therefore my soul lay out of sight,
    Untuned, unstrung:
My feeble spirit, unable to look right,
    Like a nipt blossom, hung
    Discontented.

O cheer and tune my heartless breast,
    Defer no time;
That so thy favours granting my request,
    They and my mind may chime,
    And mend my rhyme.[74]

* * *

Sum up at night, what thou hast done by day;
And in the morning what thou hast to do.
Dress and undress thy soul: mark the decay
And growth of it: if with thy watch, that too
    Be down, then wind up both; since we shall be
    Most surely judged, make thy accounts agree.[75]

Prayer at Compline Time

The day is spent, & hath His will one me:
    I and the Sun have run our races,
I went the slower, yet more paces,
    for I decay, not he.

Lord make my losses up & set me free:
    That I who cannot now by day
    Look on his daring brightness, may
        Shine then more bright than he.

If Thou defer this light, then shadow me:
    Least that the night, earth's gloomy shade
    fouling her nest, my earth invade,
        As if shades knew not Thee.

But Thou art light & darkness both together:
    If that be dark we can not see:
    The sun is darker than a tree,
        And thou more dark than either.

Yet Thou are not so dark, since I know this,
    But that my darkness may touch Thine:
    And hope, that may teach it to shine,
        Since light thy darkness is.

O let my soul, whose keys I must deliver
   Into the hands of senseless dreams
   Which know not Thee; such in Thy beams
   And wake with Thee for ever.[76]

Sacramental Devotions

Come ye hither all, whose taste
           Is your waste;
Save your cost, and mend your fare.
God is here prepared and dress'd
           And the feast.
God, in whom all dainties are.

Come ye hither all, whom wine
           Doth define,
Naming you not to your good:
Weep what ye have drunk amiss,
           And drink this,
Which before ye drink is blood.[77]

* * *

Welcome sweet and sacred cheer,
           Welcome dear;
With me, in me, live and dwell:
For thy neatness passeth sight,
           Thy delight
Passeth tongue to taste or tell.

O what sweetness from the bowl
           Fills my soul,
Such as is, and makes divine!
Is some state (fled from the sphere)
           Melted there,
As we sugar melt in wine?

Or hath a sweetness in the bread
           Make a head

To subdue the smell of sin;
Flowers, and gums, and powders giving
   All their living,
Lest the enemy should win?

Doubtless, neither star nor flower
   Hath the power
Such a sweetness to impart:
Only God, who gives perfumes,
   Flesh assumes,
And with it perfumes my heart.

But as Pomanders and wood
   Still are good,
Yet being bruised are better scented;
God, to show how far his love
   Could improve,
Her, as broken, is presented.

When I had forgot my birth,
   And on earth
In delights of earth was drown'd;
God took blood, and needs would be
   Spilt with me,
And so found me on the ground.

Having raised me to look up,
   In a cup
Sweetly he doth meet my taste.
But I still being low and short,
   Far from court,
Wine becomes a wing at last.

For with it alone I fly,
   To the sky:
Where I wipe mine eyes, and see
What I seek, for what I sue;
   Him a view,
Who hath done so much for me.

Let the wonder of this pity
   Be my ditty,

And take up my lines and life:
Hearken under pain of death,
    Hands and breath;
Strive in this, and love the strife.[78]

* * *

  O Gracious Lord, how shall I know
  Whether in these gifts Thou be so,
    As Thou art everywhere;
Or rather so, as Thou alone
Tak'st all the lodging, leaving none
    For thy poor creature there?

First I am sure, whether bread stay
Or whether Bread do fly away
    Concerneth bread, not me.
But that both Thou and all Thy train
Be there, to Thy truth & my gain,
    Concerneth me and Thee.

And if in coming to Thy foes
Thou dost come first to them, that shows
    The hast of Thy good will.
Or if that Thou two stations makest
In Bread & me the way Thou takest
    Is more, but for me still.

Then of this also I am sure
That Thou didst all those pains endure
    To' abolish sin, not Wheat.
Creatures are good, & have their place;
Sin only, which did all deface,
    Thou drivest from his seat.

I could believe an Impanation[79]
At the rate of an Incarnation,
    If Thou hadst died for Bread.
But that which made my soul to die
My flesh & fleshly villainy,
    That all so made Thee dead.

That flesh is there, mine eyes deny:

And what should flesh but flesh descry,
　　The noblest sense of five?
If glorious bodies pass the sight
Shall they be food & strength, & might
　　Even there, where they deceive?

Into my soul this cannot pass;
flesh (though exalted) keeps his grass
　　And cannot turn to soul.
Bodies and minds are different spheres
Nor can they change their bounds and meres,
　　But keep a constant pole.

This gift of all gifts is the best,
Thy flesh the least that I request.
　　Thou took'st that pledge from me:
Give me not that I had before,
Or give me that, so I have more
　　My God, give me all Thee.[80]

* * *

　　Not in rich furniture, or fine array,
　　　Nor in a wedge of gold,
　　　Thou, who for me was sold,
　　To me dost now Thy self convey;
　　For so Thou shouldst without me still have been,
　　　Leaving within me sin;

　　But by the way of nourishment and strength,
　　　Thou creep'st into my breast;
　　　Making thy way my rest,
　　And thy small quantities my length;
　　Which spread their forces into every part,
　　　Meeting sin's force and art.

　　Yet can these not get over to my soul,
　　　Leaping the wall that parts
　　　Our souls and fleshly hearts;
　　But as the out-works, they may control
　　My rebel-flesh, and carrying thy name,
　　　Affright both sin and shame.

Only thy grace, which with these elements comes,
  Knoweth the ready way,
  And has the privy key,
 Opening the souls most subtile rooms;
While those to spirits refined, at door attend
  Dispatches from their friend.

* * *

Give me my captive soul, or take
  My body also thither.
Another lift like this will make
  Them both to be together.

Before that sin turn'd flesh to stone,
  And all our lump to leaven;
A fervent sigh might well have blown
  Our innocent earth to heaven.

...

Thou hast restored us to this ease
  By this Thy heavenly blood,
Which I can go to, when I please,
  And leave the earth to their food.[81]

* * *

A broken altar, Lord, thy servant rears,
Made of a heart, and cemented with tears:
  Whose parts are as thy hand did frame;
  No workman's tool has touched the same.
    A heart alone
    Is such a stone,
    As nothing but
    Thy power doth cut.
    Wherefore each part
    Of my hard heart
    Meets in this frame,
    To praise thy Name:
  That, if I chance to hold my peace,
  These stones to praise Thee may not cease.
O let thy blessed SACRIFICE be mine,
And sanctify this ALTAR to be thine.[82]

* * *

Love bade me welcome: yet my soul drew back,
        Guilty of dust and sin.
But quick-eyed Love, observing me grow slack
        From my first entrance in,
Drew nearer to me, sweetly questioning,
        If I lack'd any thing.

A guest, I answer'd, worthy to be here:
        Love said, You shall be he.
I the unkind, ungrateful? Ah my dear,
        I cannot look on Thee.
Love took my hand, and smiling did reply,
        Who made the eyes but I?

Truth, Lord, but I have marr'd them: let my shame
        Go where it does deserve.
And know you not, says Love, who bore the blame?
        My dear, then I will serve.
You must sit down, says Love, and taste my meat:
        So I did sit and eat.[83]

The Christian Year

The Annunciation

Like Mary, help me Lord to possess a virtuous soul.

Sweet Day, so cool, so calm, so bright,
The bridal of the earth and sky,
The dew shall weep thy fall to night;
    For thou must die.

Sweet Rose, whose hue angry and brave
Bids the rash gazer wipe his eye:
Thy root is ever in its grave,
    And thou must die.

Sweet Spring, full of sweet days and roses,
A box where sweets compacted lie;
My music shows ye have your closes,
    And all must die.

Only a sweet and virtuous soul,
Like season'd timber, never gives;
But though the whole world turn to coal
    Then chiefly lives.[84]

May the holy maid be my model in honouring the Saviour of the world.
Be my friend and intercessor.

Not out of envy or maliciousness,
Do I forbear to crave your special aid.
                    I would address
My vows to thee most gladly, blessed Maid,
And Mother of my God, in my distress:

Thou art the holy Mine, whence came the Gold,
The great restorative for all decay
                    In young and old;
Thou art the cabinet where the jewel lay:
Chiefly to thee would I my soul unfold.[85]

Advent

The Beginning of the Christian Year

For Christians Paradise is the goal.

    O that I once past changing were,
Fast in thy Paradise, where no flower can wither!
    Many a spring I shoot up fair,
Offring at heaven, growing and groaning thither:
        Nor doth my flower
        Want a spring-shower,
    My sins and I joining together.

...

    And now in age I bud again,
After so many deaths I live and write;
    I once more smell the dew and rain,
And relish versing: O my only light,
        It cannot be
        That I am he
    On whom thy tempests fell at night.

    These are thy wonders, Lord of love,
To make us see we are but flowers that glide:
    Which when we once can find and prove,

Thou hast a garden for us, where to bide,
     Who would be more,
     Swelling through store,
Forfeit their Paradise by their pride.[86]

Advent is a time for reflecting on the Four Last Things.

Thoughts on judgment:

Thy life is God's, thy time to come is gone,
     And is His right.
He is thy night at noon: He is at night
     Thy noon alone.
The crop is His, for He hath sown.

And well it was for thee, when this befell,
     That God did make
Thy business His, and in thy life partake:
     For thou canst tell,
     If it be his once, all is well.

...

Things present shrink and die: but they that spend
     Their thoughts and sense
On future grief, do not remove it thence,
     But it extend,
     And draw the bottom out an end.[87]

Almighty Judge, how shall poor wretches brook
     Thy dreadful look,
Able a heart of iron to appal,
     When Thou shalt call
     For every man's peculiar book?

What others mean to do, I know not well;
     Yet I hear tell,
That some will turn Thee to some leaves therein
     So void of sin,

That they in merit shall excel.

But I resolve, when Thou shalt call for mine,
That to decline,
And thrust a Testament into thy hand:
Let that be scann'd
There Thou shalt find my faults are thine.[88]

Thoughts on death:

Death, thou wast an uncouth hideous thing,
Nothing but bones,
The sad effect of sadder groans:
Thy mouth was open, but thou couldst not sing.

...

For we do now behold thee gay and glad,
As at doomsday;
When souls shall wear their new array,
And all thy bones with beauty shall be clad.

Therefore we can go die as sleep, and trust
Half that we have
Unto an honest faithful grave;
Making our pillows either down, or dust.[89]

Thoughts on heaven:

O who will show me those delights on high?
ECHO.   I.
Thou Echo, thou art mortal, all men know.
ECHO.   No.
Were you not born among the trees and leaves?
ECHO.   Leaves.
And are there any leaves that still abide?
ECHO.   Bide.
What leaves are they? impart the matter wholly.
ECHO.   Holy

Are holy leaves the Echo then of bliss?
ECHO.   Yes.
Then tell me, what is that supreme delight?
ECHO.   Light.
Light to the mind: what shall we enjoy?
ECHO.   Joy.
But are there cares and business with the pleasure?
ECHO.   Leisure.
Light, joy, and leisure; but will they persevere?
ECHO.   Ever.[90]

Christmas

Let me also be a traveller to the Manger –

All after pleasures as I ride one day,
    My horse and I, both tired, body and mind,
    With full cry of affections, quite astray;
I took up in the next inn I could find.

There when I came, whom found I but my dear,
    My dearest Lord, expecting till the grief
    Of pleasures brought me to him, ready there
To be all passengers' most sweet relief?

O Thou, whose glorious, yet contracted light,
    Wrapt in night's mantle, stole into a manger;
    Since my dark soul and brutish is Thy right,
To Man of all beasts be not Thou a stranger.

          Furnish and deck my soul, that Thou mayst have
          A better lodging, than a rack, or grave.[91]

*Let me sing my praises in the same heartfelt fashion of the simple
shepherds.*

The shepherds sing; and shall I silent be?

My God, no hymn for Thee?
My soul's a shepherd too: a flock it feeds
      Of thoughts, and words, and deeds.
The pasture is Thy word; the streams, Thy grace
      Enriching all the place.
Shepherd and flock shall sing, and all my powers
      Out-sing the daylight hours.
Then we will chide the Sun for letting night
      Take up his place and right:
We sing one common Lord; wherefore he should
      Himself the candle hold.
I will go searching, till I find a Sun
      Shall stay, till we have done;
A willing shiner, that shall shine as gladly,
      As frost-nipt Suns look sadly.
Then we will sing, and shine all our own day,
      And one another pay:
His beams shall cheer my breast, and both so twine,
Till even his beams sing, and my music shine.[92]

Let me follow the shepherds, and also honour the King in His cratch.

Shepherds are honest people; let them sing:
Riddle who list, for me, and pull for Prime:
I envy no man's nightingale or spring;
Nor let them punish me with loss of rhyme,
Who plainly say, *My God, My King.*[93]

Lent

May I be resolute to keep this holy season as a time to grow in living in Christ, and for Christ.

Welcome dear feast of Lent: who loves not thee,
He loves not Temperance, or Authority,
      But is composed of passion.

The Scriptures bid us *fast*; the Church says, *Now*
Give to thy Mother, what thou wouldst allow
      To every Corporation.

The humble soul, composed of love and fear,
Begins at home, and lays the burden there,
      When doctrines disagree:
He says, In things which use hath justly got,
I am a scandal to the Church, and not
      The Church is so to me.

True Christians should be glad of an occasion
To use their temperance, seeking no evasion,
      When good is seasonable;
Unless Authority, which should increase
The obligation in us, make it less,
      And power itself disable.

Besides the cleanness of sweet abstinence,
Quick thoughts and motions at a small expense,
      A face not fearing light:
Whereas in fullness there are sluttish fumes,
Sour exhalations, and dishonest rheums,
      Revenging the delight.

Then those same pendant profits, which the spring
And Easter intimate, enlarge the thing,
      And goodness of the deed.
Neither ought other men's abuse of Lent
Spoil the good use; lest by that argument
      We forfeit all our Creed.

'Tis true, we cannot reach Christ's fortieth day;
Yet to go part of that religious way
      Is better than to rest:
We cannot reach our Saviour's purity;
Yet are we bid, *Be holy e'en as he.*
      In both let's do our best.

Who goeth in the way which Christ hath gone,
Is much more sure to meet with him, than one
      That travelleth by-ways.

Perhaps my God, though He be far before,
May turn, and take me by the hand, and more
       May strengthen my decays.

Yet, Lord, instruct us to improve our fast
By starving sin, and taking such repast
       As may our faults control:
That every man may revel at his door,
Not in his parlour; banqueting the poor,
       And among those his soul.[94]

Make me faithful this Lent.

       Full of rebellion, I would die,
       Or fight, or travel, or deny,
       That Thou hast ought to do with me.
                     O tame my heart;
                  · It is Thy highest art
       To captivate strong holds to Thee.

       If Thou shalt let this venom lurk,
       And in suggestions fume and work,
       My soul will turn to bubbles straight,
                     And thence by kind
                  Vanish into a wind,
       Making Thy workmanship deceit.

       O smooth my rugged heart, and there
       Engrave Thy reverend law and fear;
       Or make a new one, since the old
                     Is sapless grown,
                  And a much fitter stone
       To hide my dust, then Thee to hold.[95]

                     * * *

       But man is close, reserved, and dark to Thee:
              When Thou demandest but a heart,
                  He cavils instantly.
              In his poor cabinet of bone
                  Sins have their box apart,
       Defrauding Thee, who gavest two for one.[96]

Help me to admit my sins and to see myself as God knows me.

Only an open breast
Doth shut them out, so they cannot enter;
Or, if they enter, cannot rest,
But quickly seek some new adventure.
Smooth open hearts no fasting have; but fiction
Doth give a hold and handle to affliction.

Wherefore my faults and sins,
Lord, I acknowledge; take thy plagues away;
For since confession pardon wins,
I challenge here the brightest day,
The clearest diamond: let them do their best
They shall be thick and cloudy to my breast.[97]

The mockery of sin, let it never confound me.

Indeed at first Man was a treasure,
A box of jewels, shop of rarities,
A ring, whose posy was, *My Pleasure*:
He was a garden in a Paradise:
Glory and grace
Did crown his heart and face.

But sin hath fool'd him. Now he is
A lump of flesh, without a foot or wing
To raise him to the glimpse of bliss:
A sick toss'd vessel, dashing on each thing;
Nay, his own shelf:
My God, I mean myself.[98]

Help me, Lord, in my temptations so that they do not turn to sin.

Before that sin turn'd flesh to stone.
And all our lump to leaven;
A fervent sigh might well have blown
Our innocent earth to heaven.

For sure Adam did not know
    To sin, or sin to smother;
He might to heaven from Paradise go,
    As from one room to another.[99]

Do not leave me comfortless, despite my sins, O Lord.

O do not use me
After my sins! look not on my desert,
But on thy glory! then Thou wilt reform,
And not refuse me: for Thou only art
The mighty God, but I a silly worm;
    O do not bruise me!

    O do not urge me!
For what account can thy ill steward make?
I have abused Thy stock, destroy'd Thy woods,
Suck'd all Thy magazines: my head did ache,
Till it found out how to consume Thy goods:
    O do not scourge me!

    O do not blind me!
I have deserved that an Egyptian night
Should thicken all my powers; because my lust
Hath still sow'd fig-leaves to exclude thy light:
But I am frailty, and already dust;
    O do not grind me!

    O do not fill me
With the turn'd vial of Thy bitter wrath!
For Thou hast other vessels full of blood,
A part whereof my Saviour emptied hath,
Even unto death: since He died for my good,
    O do not kill me!

    But O, reprieve me!
For Thou hast *life*, and *death* at Thy command;
Thou are both *Judge* and *Saviour*, *Feast* and *Rod*,
Cordial and *Corrosive*: put not Thy hand
Into the bitter box; but, O my God,
    My God, relieve me![100]

In my foolishness I so often choose sin rather than virtue:

> Lord, let the Angels praise Thy name.
> Man is a foolish thing, a foolish thing,
>   Folly and Sin play all his game.
> His house still burns; and yet he still doth sing,
>   *Man is but grass,*
>   *He knows it, fill the glass.*

...

>   Man cannot serve Thee; let him go,
> And serve the swine: there, there is his delight:
>   He doth not like this virtue, no;
> Give him his dirt to wallow in all night;
>   These Preachers make
>   His head to shoot and ache.[101]

Let me truly accept the cost of my sin.

> I know it is my sin, which locks Thine ears.
>   And binds Thy hands,
> Out-crying my requests, drowning my tears;
> Or else the chillness of my faint demands.
>
> But as cold hands are angry with the fire,
>   And mend it still;
> So I do lay the want of my desire,
> Not on my sins, or coldness, but Thy will.
>
> Yet hear, O God, only for His blood's sake,
>   Which pleads for me:
> For though sins plead too, yet like stones they make
> His blood's sweet current much more loud to be.[102]

Help me to know that repentance means turning – turning away from sin and turning to God – 'turn right round'.

> Sorry I am, my God, sorry I am,
> That my offences course it in a ring.

My thoughts are working like a busy flame,
Until their cockatrice they hatch and bring:
And when they once have perfected their draughts,
My words take fire from my inflamed thoughts.

My words take fire from my inflamed thoughts,
Which spit it forth like the Sicilian Hill.
They vent the wares, and pass them with their faults,
And by their breathing ventilate the ill.
But words suffice not, where are lewd intentions:
My hands do join to finish the inventions:

My hands do join to finish the inventions:
And so my sins ascend three stories high,
As Babel grew, before there were dissensions.
Yet ill deeds loiter not: for they supply
New thoughts of sinning; wherefore, to my shame,
Sorry I am, my God, sorry I am.[103]

*Help me, dear Lord, to search my being each day, and to acknowledge
all my sins, and how I have failed you.*

Lord, I confess my sin is great;
Great is my sin. Oh! Gently treat
With thy quick flower, thy momentary bloom;
Whose life still pressing
Is one undressing,
A steady aiming at a tomb.

Man's age is two hours' work, or three:
Each day doth round about us see.
Thus are we to delights: but we are all
To sorrows old,
If life be told
From what life feeleth, Adam's fall.

O let Thy height of mercy then
Compassionate short-breathed men.
Cut me off from my most foul transgression:
I do confess

My foolishness;
My God, accept of my confession.

Sweeten at length this bowl,
Which Thou hast pour'd into my soul;
Thy wormwood turns to health, winds to fair weather:
For if Thou stay,
I and this day,
As we did rise, we die together.

When Thou for sin rebukest man,
Forwith he waxeth woe and wan:
Bitterness fills our bowels; all our hearts
Pine, and decay,
And drop away,
And carry with them the other parts.

But Thou wilt sin and grief destroy;
That so the broken bones may joy,
And tune together in a well-set song,
Full of his praises,
Who dead men raises.
Fractures well cured make us more strong.[104]

Holy Week

One way of meditating on The Passion *is by using* The Sacrifice. *This long poem has appropriate breaking points to make it easier for use during Holy Week.*

Oh all ye, who pass by, whose eyes and mind
To worldly things are sharp, but to me blind;
To Me, who took eyes that I might you find:
Was ever grief like Mine?

The Princes of My people make a head
Against their Maker: they do wish Me dead,
Who cannot wish, except I give them bread:
Was ever grief like Mine?

Without Me each one, who doth now Me brave,
Had to this day been an Egyptian slave.
They use that power against Me, which I gave:
    Was ever grief like Mine?

Mine own Apostle, who the bag did bear,
Though he had all I had, did not forbear
To sell Me also, and to put Me there:
    Was ever grief like Mine?

For thirty pence he did My death devise
Who at three hundred did the ointment prize,
Not half so sweet as My sweet sacrifice:
    Was ever grief like Mine?

* * *

Therefore My soul melts, and My hearts dear treasure
Drops blood (the only beads) My words to measure:
O let this cup pass, if it be Thy pleasure:
    Was ever grief like Mine?

These drops being temper'd with a sinner's tears,
A Balsam are for both the Hemispheres,
Curing all wounds, but Mine; all, but my fears.
    Was ever grief like Mine?

Yet My Disciples sleep: I cannot gain
One hour of watching; but their drowsy brain
Comforts not Me, and doth My doctrine stain;
    Was ever grief like Mine?

Arise, arise, they come. Look how they run!
Alas! What haste they make to be undone!
How with their lanterns do they seek the Sun!
    Was ever grief like Mine?

With clubs and staves they seek Me, as a thief,
Who am the way of truth, the true relief,
Most true to those who are my greatest grief:
    Was ever grief like Mine?

* * *

Judas, dost thou betray Me with a kiss?

Canst thou find hell about My lips? and miss
Of life, just as the gates of life and bliss?
Was ever grief like Mine?

See, they lay hold on Me, not with the hands
Of faith, but fury; yet at their commands
I suffer binding, who have loosed their bands:
Was ever grief like Mine?

All My Disciples fly; fear puts a bar
Betwixt my friends and Me. They leave the star,
That brought the wise men of the East from far.
Was ever grief like Mine?

* * *

Then from one ruler to another bound
They lead Me: urging, that it was not sound
What I taught: Comments would the text confound.
Was ever grief like Mine?

The priests and rulers all false witness seek
'Gainst him, who seeks not life, but is the meek
And ready Paschal Lamb of this great week:
Was ever grief like Mine?

They accuse Me of great blasphemy,
That I did thrust into the Deity,
Who never thought that any robbery:
Was ever grief like Mine?

Some said, that I the Temple to the floor
In three days razed, and raised as before.
Why, He who built the world can do much more:
Was ever grief like Mine?

Then they condemn Me all with that same breath,
Which I do give them daily, unto death.
Thus *Adam* my first breathing rendereth:
Was ever grief like Mine?

* * *

They bind, and lead Me unto *Herod*: he
Sends Me to *Pilate*. This makes them agree;

But yet their relationship is My enmity.
  Was ever grief like Mine?

Herod and all his bands do set Me light.
Who teach all hands to war, fingers to fight,
And only am the Lord of Hosts and might:
  Was ever grief like Mine?

Herod in judgment sits, while I do stand;
Examines Me with a censorious hand:
I him obey, who all things else command:
  Was ever grief like Mine?

* * *

The *Jews* accuse Me with despitefulness;
And vying malice with My gentleness,
Pick quarrels with their only happiness:
  Was ever grief like Mine?

I answer nothing, but with patience prove
If stony hearts will melt with gentle love,
But who does hawk at eagles with a dove?
  Was ever grief like Mine?

My silence rather does augment their cry;
My dove doth back into my bosom fly,
Because the raging waters still are high:
  Was ever grief like Mine?

Hark how they cry aloud still, *Crucify*:
It is not fit he live a day, they cry,
Who cannot live less then eternally:
  Was ever grief like Mine?

Pilate, a stranger, holdeth off; but they,
Mine own dear people, cry, *Away, Away*,
With noises confused frightening the day:
  Was ever grief like Mine?

Yet still they shout, and cry, and stop their ears,
Putting my life among their sins and fears,
And therefore with *My blood on them and theirs*:
  Was ever grief like Mine?

See how spite cankers things. These words aright
Used, and wished, are the whole world's delight:
But honey is their gall, brightness their night:
>   *Was ever grief like Mine?*

They choose a murderer, and all agree
In him to do themselves a courtesy:
For it was their own case who killed me:
>   *Was ever grief like Mine?*

And a seditious murderer he was:
But I the Prince of peace; peace that doth pass
All understanding, more than heaven doth glass:
>   *Was ever grief like Mine?*

* * *

Why, Caesar is their only King, not I:
He clave the stony rock, when they were dry;
But surely not their hearts, as I well try:
>   *Was ever grief like Mine?*

Ah, how they scourge Me! yet My tenderness
Doubles each lash: and yet their bitterness
Winds up my grief to a mysteriousness:
>   *Was ever grief like Mine?*

They buffet Me, and box Me as they list,
Who grasp the earth and heaven with my fist,
And never yet, whom I would punish, miss'd:
>   *Was ever grief like Mine?*

Behold, they spit on Me in scornful wise,
Who by My spittle gave the blind man eyes,
Leaving his blindness to My enemies:
>   *Was ever grief like Mine?*

My face they cover, though it be divine.
As *Moses'* face was veiled, so is Mine,
Lest on their double-dark souls either shine:
>   *Was ever grief like Mine?*

Servants and abjects flout Me; they are witty:

Now prophecy who strikes thee, is their ditty.
So they in Me deny themselves all pity:
     Was ever grief like Mine?

And now I am deliver'd unto death,
Which each one calls for so with utmost breath,
That he before Me well nigh suffereth:
     Was ever grief like Mine?

Weep not, dear friends, since I for both hath wept
When all My tears were blood, the while you slept:
Your tears for your own fortunes should be kept:
     Was ever grief like Mine?

* * *

The soldiers lead Me to the common hall;
There they deride Me, they abuse Me all;
Yet for twelve heavenly legions I could call:
     Was ever grief like Mine?

Then with a scarlet robe they Me array;
Which shows My blood to be the only way
And cordial left to repair man's decay:
     Was ever grief like Mine?

Then on My head a crown of thorns I wear:
For these are all the grapes Sion doth bear,
Though I My vine planted and water'd there:
     Was ever grief like Mine?

So sits the earth's great curse in Adam's fall
Upon my head: so I remove it all
From the earth unto my brows, and bear the thrall:
     Was ever grief like Mine?

* * *

Then with the reed they gave to me before,
They strike my head, the rock from whence all store
Of heav'nly blessings issue evermore:
     Was ever grief like Mine?

They bow their knees to me, and cry, Hail King:

Whatever scoffs or scornfulness can bring,
I am the floor, the sink, where they it fling:
  Was ever grief like Mine?

Yet since man's sceptres are as frail as reeds,
And thorny all their crowns, bloody their weeds;
I, who am Truth, turn into truth their deeds:
  Was ever grief like Mine?

   * * *

The soldiers also spit upon that face
Which angels did desire to have the grace,
And prophets once to see, but found no place:
  Was ever grief like Mine?

Thus trimmed, forth they bring Me to the rout,
Who *Crucify him*, cry with one strong shout.
God holds his peace at man, and man cries out:
  Was ever grief like Mine?

They lead Me in once more, and putting then
My own clothes on, they lead Me out again.
Whom devils fly, thus is he toss'd of men:
  Was ever grief like Mine?

And now weary of sport, glad to engross
All spite in one, counting My life their loss,
They carry Me to My most bitter cross:
  Was ever grief like Mine?

   * * *

My cross I bear Myself, until I faint:
Then Simon bears it for me by constraint,
The decreed burden of each mortal Saint:
  Was ever grief like Mine?

O all ye who pass by, behold and see:
Man stole the fruit, but I must climb the tree;
The tree of life to all, but only Me:
  Was ever grief like Mine?

Lo, here I hang, charged with a world of sin,

The greater world o' the two; for that came in
By words, but this by sorrow I must win:
> *Was ever grief like Mine?*

Such sorrow, as if sinful man could feel,
Or feel his part, he would not cease to kneel,
Till all were melted, though he were all steel:
> *Was ever grief like Mine?*

* * *

But, *O my God, my God*! why leavest Thou Me,
That Son, in whom Thou dost delight to be?
My God, My God _____
> *Never was grief like Mine?*

Shame tears My soul, My body many a wound;
Sharp nails pierce this, but sharper that confound;
Reproaches, which are free, while I am bound:
> *Was ever grief like Mine?*

Now heal thy self, Physician; now come down.
Alas! I did so, when I left My crown
And Father's smile for you, to feel his frown:
> *Was ever grief like Mine?*

In healing not Myself, there doth consist
All that salvation, which ye now resist;
Your safety in My sickness doth subsist:
> *Was ever grief like Mine?*

Betwixt two thieves I spend my utmost breath,
As He who for some robbery suffereth.
Alas! what have I stolen from you? Death:
> *Was ever grief like Mine?*

A king my title is, prefixed on high;
Yet My subjects I'm condemn'd to die
A servile death in servile company:
> *Was ever grief like Mine?*

They give Me vinegar mingled with gall,
But more with malice: yet, when they did call,

With Manna, Angels' food, I fed them all:
    Was ever grief like Mine?

They part My garments, and by lot dispose
My coat, the type of love, which once cured those
Who sought for help, never malicious foes:
    Was ever grief like Mine?

Nay, after death their spite shall further go;
For they will pierce My side, I full well know;
That as sin came, so Sacraments might flow:
    Was ever grief like Mine?

But now I die; now all is finished.
My woe, man's weal: and now I bow my head.
Only let others say, when I am dead,
    Never was grief like Mine?[105]

Good Friday

*Can I ever comprehend the immensity of Christ's act, or will my grief
ever be sufficient for my Lord's sufferings?*

O my chief good,
      How shall I measure out Thy blood?
How shall I count what Thee befell,
      And each grief tell?

    Shall I thy woes
Number according to Thy foes?
Or since one star show'd Thy first breath,
      Shall all Thy death?

    Or shall each leaf,
Which falls in Autumn, score a grief?
Or cannot leaves, but fruit, be sign
      Of the true vine?

    Then let each hour
Of my whole life one grief devour;

That thy distress through all may run,
    And be my sun.[106]

I can only know Christ through the Cross; there is no other way.

Having been tenant long to a rich Lord,
    Not thriving, I resolved to be bold,
    And make a suit unto Him, to afford
A new small-rented lease, and cancel the old.

In heaven at his manor I Him sought:
    They told me there, that He was lately gone
    About some land, which he had dearly bought
Long since on earth, to take possession.

I straight return'd, and knowing His great birth,
    Sought Him accordingly in great resorts; ·
    In cities, theatres, gardens, parks, and courts:
At length I heard a ragged noise and mirth
    Of thieves and murderers: there I Him espied,
    Who straight, *Your suit is granted*, said and died.[107]

The challenge of the Cross is exacting and prodding.

What is this strange and uncouth thing
To make me sigh, and seek, and faint and die,
Until I had some place, where I might sing,
    And serve Thee; and not only I,
But all my wealth, and family might combine
To set thy honour up, as our design.

    And then when after much delay,
Much wrestling, many a combat, this dear end,
So much desired, is given, to take away
    My power to serve Thee: to unbend
All my abilities, my designs confound,
And lay my threatenings bleeding on the ground.[108]

I too condemn our dear Lord to Golgotha.

Thou who condemnest Jewish hate,
For choosing Barabbas a murderer
    Before the Lord of Glory;
Look back upon thine own estate,
Call home thine eye (that busy wanderer)
    That choice may be thy story.

He that doth love, and love amiss
This world's delights before true Christian joy,
    Hath made a Jewish choice:
The world an ancient murderer is;
Thousands of souls it hath and doth destroy
    With her enchanting voice.

He that hath made a sorry wedding
Between his soul and gold, and hath preferr'd
    False gain before the true,
Hath done what he condemns in reading:
For he hath sold for money His dear Lord,
    And is a Judas-Jew.

Thus we prevent the last great day,
And judge ourselves. That light, which sin and passion
    Did before dim and choke,
When once those snuffles are ta'en away,
Shines bright and clear, e'en unto condemnation,
    Without excuse or cloke.[109]

Help me, Lord, to renew my devotion to the Suffering Christ.

Lord, I am Thine, and Thou art mine:
So mine Thou art, that something more
I may presume Thee mine, than Thine.
For Thou didst suffer to restore
Not Thee, but me, and to be mine:
And with advantage mine the more,
Since Thou in death wast none of Thine,
Yet then as mine didst me restore.
    O be mine still! still make me Thine!
    Or rather make no Thine and Mine![110]

Easter I

May I celebrate the joys of Easter as expressed through the music of nature and the rising sun.

Rise heart, Thy Lord is risen. Sing His praise
        Without delays,
Who takes thee by the hand, that thou likewise
        With Him mayst rise:
That, as His death calcined thee to dust,
His life may make thee gold, and much more, just.

Awake, my lute, and struggle for thy part
        With all thy art.
The cross taught all wood to resound his name,
        Who bore the same.
His stretched sinews taught all strings, what key
Is best to celebrate this most high day.

Consort both heart and lute, and twist a song
        Pleasant and long:
Or, since all music is but three parts vied,
        And multiplied,
O let Thy blessed Spirit bear a part,
And make up our defects with his sweet art.

I got me flowers to straw Thy way;
I got me boughs off many a tree:
But Thou wast up by break of day,
And brought'st thy sweets along with thee.

The Sun arising in the East,
Though he give light, and the East perfume;
If they should offer to contest
With Thy arising, they presume.

Can there be any day but this,
Though many suns to shine endeavour?
We count three hundred, and we miss:
There is but one, and that one ever.[111]

The resurrection means I can be as free as the lark, and rise above all earthly ties. Like the lark too, may I always sing my praises to the Risen Lord.

Lord, who createdst man in wealth and store,
Though foolishly he lost the same,
Decaying more and more,
Till be became
Most poor:

With Thee
O let me rise
As larks, harmoniously,
And sing this day Thy victories:
Then shall the fall further the flight in me.

My tender age in sorrow did begin:
And still with sicknesses and shame
Thou didst so punish sin,
That I became
Most thin,

With Thee
Let me combine,
And feel this day Thy victory:
For, if I imp my wing on Thine,
Affliction shall advance the flight in me.[112]

Christ's victory wipes away all our tears because His victory can also be ours.

Awake sad heart, who sorrow ever drowns;
Take up thine eyes, which feed on earth;
Unfold thy forehead gather'd into frowns:
Thy Saviour comes, and with Him mirth:
Awake, awake;
And with a thankful heart His comforts take.
But thou dost still lament, and pine and cry;
And feel His death, but not His victory.

Arise sad heart; if thou do not withstand,
   Christ's resurrection thine may be:
Do not by hanging down break from the hand,
   Which as it riseth, raiseth thee:
           Arise, arise;
And with his burial-linen dry thine eyes.
   Christ left his grave-clothes, that we might when grief
Draw tears, or blood, not want a handkerchief.[113]

Easter III

Good Shepherd Sunday

The God of love my shepherd is,
   And He that doth me feed:
While He is mine, and I am His,
   What can I want or need?

He leads me to the tender grass,
   Where I both feed and rest;
Then to the streams that gently pass:
   In both I have the best.

Or if I stray, He doth convert,
   And bring my mind in frame:
And all this not for my desert,
   But for His holy name.

Yea, in death's shady black abode
   Well may I walk, not fear:
For Thou art with me, and Thy rod
   To guide, Thy staff to bear.

Nay, Thou dost make me sit and dine,
   E'en in my enemies' sight;
My head with oil, my cup with wine
   Runs over day and night.

Surely Thy sweet and wondrous love

Shall measure all my days;
And as it never shall remove,
So neither shall my praise.[114]

Pentecost

Fill me Lord with that fire which burned within the apostles on the first Pentecost morning.

Listen, sweet Dove unto my song,
And spread Thy golden wings in me;
Hatching my tender heart so long,
Till it get wing, and fly away with Thee.

Where is that fire which once descended
On Thy Apostles? Thou didst then
Keep open house, richly attended,
Feasting all comers by twelve chosen men.

Such glorious gifts Thou didst bestow,
That the earth did like a heaven appear:
The stars were coming down to know
If they might mend their wages, and serve here.

The Sun, which once did shine alone,
Hung down his head, and wish'd for night,
When he beheld twelve Suns for one
Going about the world, and giving light.

But since those pipes of gold, which brought
That cordial water to our ground,
Were cut and martyr'd by the fault
Of those, who did themselves thro' their side wound;

Thou shutt'st the door, and keep'st within;
Scarce a good joy creeps through the chink:
And if the braves of conquering sin
Did not excite Thee, we should wholly sink.

Lord, though we change, Thou art the same;

The same sweet God of love and light:
Restore this day, for Thy great Name,
Unto his ancient and miraculous right.[115]

May your grace act as the dew and cleanse me from all my dross.

My stock lies dead, and no increase
Doth my dull husbandry improve:
O let thy graces without cease
    Drop from above!

If still the Sun should hide his face,
Thy house would but a dungeon prove,
Thy works night's captives: O let grace
    Drop from above!

The dew doth every morning fall;
And shall the dew out-strip Thy Dove?
The dew, for which grass cannot call,
    Drop from above.

Death is still working like a mole,
And digs my grave at each remove:
Let grace work too, and on my soul
    Drop from above.

Sin is still hammering my heart
Upon a hardness, void of love:
Let suppling grace, to cross his art,
    Drop from above.

O come! for Thou dost know the way.
Or if to me Thou wilt not move,
Remove me, where I need not say,
    Drop from above.[116]

Trinity

May I praise God for all His love as expressed in his continued creativity, redemption and strengthening.

Lord, who hast form'd me out of mud,
    And hast redeem'd me through Thy blood,
    And sanctified me to do good.

Purge all my sins done heretofore:
    For I confess my heavy score,
    And I will strive to sin no more.

Enrich my heart, mouth, hands in me,
    With faith, with hope, with charity;
    That I may run, rise, rest with Thee.[117]

The Angels and Saints

Mary Magdalen

Love means giving my most precious possession to my Lord.

When blessed Mary wiped her Saviour's feet,
(Whose precepts she had trampled on before)
And wore them for a Jewel on her head,
    Showing his steps should be the street,
    Wherein she thenceforth evermore
With pensive humbleness would live and tread:

She being stain'd her self, why did she strive
To make Him clean, who could not be defiled?
Why kept she not her tears for her own faults,
    And not his feet? Though we could dive
    In tears like Seas, our sins are piled
Deeper than they, in words, and works, and thoughts.

Dear soul, she knew who did vouchsafe and design
To bear her filth; and that her sins did dash
E'en God Himself: wherefore she was not loath,
    As she had brought wherewith to stain,
    So to bring in wherewith to wash:
And yet in washing one, she washed both.[118]

*To all the angels and saints, especially Our Lady. May they pray for me
as I tread my earthly pilgrimage.*

Oh glorious spirits, who after all your bands
See the smooth face of God, without a frown,
          Or strict commands;
Where every one is king, and hath his crown,
If not upon his head, yet in his hands:

Not out on envy or maliciousness
Do I forbear to crave your special aid:
          I would address
My vows to thee most gladly, blessed Maid,
And Mother of my God, in my distress.

Thou art the holy Mine, whence came the Gold,
The great restorative for all decay
          In young and old;
Thou art the Cabinet where the jewel lay:
Chiefly to thee would I my soul unfold:

But now, alas! I dare not; for our King,
Whom we do all jointly adore and praise,
          Bid no such thing:
And where his pleasure no injunction lays,
('Tis your own case) ye never move a wing.

All worship is prerogative, and a flower
Of His rich crown, from whom lies no appeal
          At the last hour:
Therefore we dare not from this garland steal,
To make a posy for inferior power.

Although then others court you, if we know
What's done on earth, we shall not fare the worse,
          Who do not so;
Since we are ever ready to disburse,
If any one our Master's hand can show.[119]

The Holy Name of Jesus

*May I pray the Jesu prayer over and over each day until Jesus penetrates
through all my egotism.*

Jesu is in my heart, His sacred name
Is deeply carved there: but the other week
A great affliction broke the little frame,
E'en all to pieces: which I went to seek:
And first I found the corner, where was J,
After, where ES, and next where U was graved.
When I had got these parcels, instantly
I sat me down to spell them, and perceived
That to my broken heart he was I ease you
            And to my whole is J E S U.[120]

Christian character

Love

Immortal Heat, O let Thy greater flame
    Attract the lesser to it: let those fires
    Which shall consume the world, first make it tame;
And kindle in our hearts such true desires,

As may consume our lusts, and make Thee way.
    Then shall our hearts pant Thee; then shall our brain
    All her invention on Thine Altar lay,
And there in hymns send back Thy fire again:

Our eyes shall see Thee, which before saw dust;
    Dust blown by wit, till that they both were blind:
    Thou shalt recover all Thy goods in kind,
Who wert disseized by usurping lust:

        All knees shall bow to Thee; all wits shall rise,
        And praise Him who did make and mend our eyes.[121]

Truth

Lie not; but let thy heart be true to God,
Thy mouth to it, thy actions to them both:
Cowards tell lies, and those that fear the rod;
The stormy working soul spits lies and froth.
    Dare to be true. Nothing can need a lie:
    A fault, which needs it most, grows two thereby.[122]

Gratefulness

Thou that hast given so much to me,
Give one thing more, a grateful heart.
See how thy beggar works on thee
    By art.

He makes thy gifts occasion more,
And says, If he in this be crost,
All thou hast giv'n him heretofore
    Is lost.

But Thou didst reckon, when at first
Thy word our hearts and hands did crave,
What it would come to at the worst,
    To save.

Perpetual knockings at Thy door,
Tears sullying Thy transparent rooms,
Gift upon gift; much would have more,
    And comes.

This notwithstanding, Thou went'st on,
And did allow us all our noise:
Nay, Thou hast made a sigh and groan
    Thy joys.

Not that Thou hast not still above
Much better tunes, than groans can make;
But that these country-airs Thy love
    Did take.

Wherefore I cry, and cry again;
And in no quiet canst thou be,
Till I a thankful heart obtain
      Of Thee:

Not thankful, when it pleases me;
As if Thy blessings had spare days:
But such a heart, whose pulse may be
      Thy praise.[123]

Thriftiness

Be thrifty, but not covetous: therefore give
Thy need, thine honour, and thy friend his due.
Never was scraper brave man. Get to live;
Then live, and use it: else, it is not true
    That thou hast gotten. Surely use alone
    Makes money not a contemptible stone.

Never exceed thy income. Youth may make
Even with the year: but age, if it will hit,
Shoots a bow short, and lessens still his stake,
As the day lessens, and his life with it,
    Thy children, kindred, friends upon Thee call;
    Before thy journey fairly part with all.[124]

Good Temper

Be sweet to all. Is thy complexion sour?
Then keep such company; make them thy allay:

...

Catch not at quarrels. He that dares not speak
Plainly and home, is coward of the two.

...

Be calm in arguing: for fierceness makes
Error a fault, and truth discourtesy.

Why should I feel another man's mistakes
More than his sicknesses or poverty?
    In love I should: but anger is not love,
    Nor wisdom neither: therefore gently move.[125]

Humility

Pitch thy behaviour low, thy projects high;
So shalt thou humble and magnanimous be:
Sink not in spirit: who aimeth at the sky
Shoots higher much then he that means a tree.
    A grain of glory mixt with humbleness
    Cures both a fever and lethargicness.

...

Scorn no man's love, though of a mean degree;
(Love is a present for a mighty king,)
Much less make any one thine enemy.
As guns destroy, so may a little sling,
    The cunning workman never doth refuse
    The meanest tool, that he may chance to use.[126]

Charity

In Alms regard thy means, and others' merit.
Think heaven a better bargain, than to give
Only thy single market-money for it.
Joins hands with God to make a man to live.
    Give to all something; to a good poor man,
    Till thou change names, and be where he began.

Man is God's image; but a poor man is
Christ's stamp to boot: both images regard.
God reckons for him, counts the favour his:
Write, *So much given to God*; thou shall be heard.
    Let thy alms go before, and keep heavens gate
    Open for Thee; or both may come too late.[127]

* * *

Be useful where thou livest, that they may
Both want and wish thy pleasing presence still.
Kindness, good parts, great places, are the way
To compass this. Find out men's wants and will,
  And meet them there. All worldly joys go less
To the one joy of doing kindnesses.[128]

Constancy

  Who is the honest man?
He who doth still and strongly good pursue,
To God, his neighbour, and himself most true:
  Whom neither force nor fawning can
Unpin, or wrench from giving all their due.

  Whose honesty is not
So loose or easy, that a ruffling wind
Can blow away, or glittering look it blind:
  Who rides his sure and even trot,
While the world now rides by, now lags behind.

  Who, when great trials come,
Nor seeks, nor shuns them; but doth calmly stay,
Till he the thing and the example weigh:
  All being brought into a sum,
What place or person calls for, he doth pay.

  Whom none can work or woo,
To use in any thing a trick or sleight;
For above all things he abhors deceit:
  His words and works and fashion too
All of a piece, and all are clear and straight.

  Who never melts or thaws
At close temptations: when the day is done,
His goodness sets not, but in dark can run:
  The sun to others writeth laws,
And is their virtue; Virtue is his Sun.

  Who, when he is to treat

With sick folks, women, those whom passions sway,
Allows for that, and keeps his constant way:
    Whom others' faults do not defeat;
But though men fail him, yet his part doth play.;

    Whom nothing can procure,
When the wide world runs bias, from his will
To writhe his limbs, and share, not mend the ill.
    This is the Marksman, safe and sure,
Who still is right, and prays to be so still.[129]

Against Lust

Beware of lust: it doth pollute and foul
Whom God in Baptism wash'd with His own blood:
It blots the lesson written in thy soul;
The holy lines cannot be understood.
    How dare those eyes upon a Bible look,
    Much less towards God, whose lust is all their book?

Wholly abstain, or wed. Thy bounteous Lord
Allows thee choice of paths: take no bye-ways;
But gladly welcome what He doth afford;
Not grudging, that thy lust has bounds and stays.
    Continence hath his joy: weigh both; and so
    If rottenness hath more, let heaven go.[130]

Against Idleness

Fly idleness, which yet thou canst not fly
By dressing, mistressing, and compliment.
If those take up thy day, the Sun will cry
Against thee: for his light was only lent.
    God gave thy soul brave wings; put not those feathers
    Into a bed, to sleep out ill weathers.[131]

Against Wealth

Wealth is the conjurer's devil;
Whom when he think he has, the devil hath him.
Gold thou mayst safely touch; but if it stick
Unto thy hands, it woundeth to the quick.

What skills it, if a bag of stones or gold
About thy neck do drown thee? raise thy head;
Take stars for money; stars not to be told
By any art, yet to be purchased.
None is so wasteful as the scraping dame.
She loseth three for one; her soul, rest, fame.[132]

Against Envy

Envy not greatness: for thou makest thereby
Thyself the worse, and so the distance greater.
Be not thine own worm: yet such jealousy,
As hurts not others, but may make thee better,
Is a good spur. Correct thy passions spite;
Then may the beasts draw thee to happy light.[133]

Against Blasphemy

Take not His name, who made thy mouth, in vain:
It gets thee nothing, and hath no excuse.
Lust and wine plead a pleasure, avarice gain:
But the cheap swearer through his open sluice
Lets his soul run for nought, as little fearing.
Were I an *Epicure*, I could bate swearing.[134]

Against Imbibing

Drink not the third glass, which thou canst not tame,
When once it is within thee; but before

Mayst rule it, as thou lift: and pour the shame,
Which it would pour on thee, upon the floor.
    It is most just to throw that on the ground,
    Which would throw me there, it I keep the round.

...

Shall I, to please another's wine-sprung mind,
Lose all mine own? God hath given me a measure
Short of his can and body; must I find
A pain in that, wherein he finds a pleasure?
    Stay at the third glass: if thou lose thy hold,
    Then thou art modest, and the wine grows bold.

...

Yet, if thou sin in wine or wantonness,
Boast not thereof; nor make thy shame thy glory.
Frailty gets pardon by submissiveness;
But he that boasts, shuts that out of his story.
    He makes flat war with God, and doth defy
    With his poor clod of earth the spacious sky.[135]

The Danger of Wit

Wit's an unruly engine, wildly striking
Sometimes a friend, sometimes the engineer.
Hast thou the knack? pamper it not with liking:
But if you want it, buy it not too dear.
    Many, affecting wit beyond their power,
    Have got to be a dear fool for an hour.[136]

Rule of Life

Who keeps no guard upon himself, is slack,
And rots to nothing at the next great thaw.
Man is a shop of rules, a well truss'd pack,
Whose every parcel under-writes a law.
    Lose not thy self, nor give thy humours way:
    God gave them to thee under lock and key.[137]

Teach me, my God and King,
In all things Thee to see,
And what I do in anything,
To do it as for Thee.[138]

Sources

1. G. Herbert, *The Works of George Herbert*, 2 vols., (London, Bell and Daldy, Fleet Street, 1859), Vol. 2, p. xxiv.
2. Ibid., pp. 126–7.
3. Ibid., p. xxvi.
4. Ibid., p. 200.
5. Ibid., pp. 185–6.
6. Ibid., p. 183.
7. Ibid., Vol. 1, p. 160, Herbert inherited his orderliness of life from his Mother. In his *Memoriae Matris Sacrum*, he described how for her that within the family, household and neighbours, and house and garden, everything must have its place, while her commitment to such as the sick and needy must be thoroughly organized, as were indeed her own religious practices.
8. Ibid., Vol. 2, p. 61. from *Matins*.
9. Ibid., p. 63. from *Even-song*.
10. Ibid., p. 64.
11. Ibid., Vol. 1, p. 178.
12. Ibid., pp. 167, 211.
13. Ibid., p. 167.
14. Ibid., Vol. 2, pp. 76–8.
15. Ibid., Vol. 1, pp. 174–5.
16. Ibid., Vol. 2, p. 183. From *The Priesthood*.
17. I. Walton, *The Life of George Herbert*, in *The Works of George Herbert*, 2 vols. (London, 1859), Vol. 1, p. 74. Hereafter referred to as Walton.

18. Ibid., p. 55.
19. Ibid., pp. 55–6.
20. Herbert, op. cit., Vol 2, p. 207. From *The Invitation*.
21. Ibid., Vol. 1, p. 187, 194, 197–8.
22. Ibid., p. 189.
23. Walton, op. cit., p. 77.
24. Herbert, op. cit., Vol. 2, p. 19. From *The Superliminare*.
25. Herbert had already repaired the church at Layton where he had been appointed as a prebend by Bishop Williams of Lincoln. When Herbert came to there he found that 'the fair church of Layton was fallen down a long time, and lay in the dust.' The cost for repairing was at least two thousand pounds. With his dear friends at Little Gidding, Nicholas and John Ferrar, he 'spared not his own purse.' John, writing to Nicholas on 30/7/1632, described the progress being made; 'We have 18 masons and labourers at work at Layton church, and we shall have this week 10 carpenters, God prosper the work and send money in Amen.' B. Blackstone (ed.), *The Ferrar Papers*, (Cambridge, 1938), pp. 58, 276.
26. Herbert, op. cit., Vol. 1, pp. 192–3.
27. Ibid., Vol. 2, p. 84. From *Christmas*.
28. Ibid., Vol. 1, pp. 166, 168.
29. Ibid., Vol. 2, p. 16. From *The Church Porch*.
30. Ibid., Vol. 1, p. 168.
31. Ibid., Vol. 2, pp. 16–17. From *The Church Porch*.
32. G. Herbert, *Herbert's Remains, or Sundry Pieces of that Sweet Singer of The Temple*, London, 1652, pp. 92–3.
33. Walton, op. cit., pp. 64, 67.
34. Herbert, op. cit., Vol. 2, p. 16, *The Church Porch*.
35. Ibid., p. 111. From *Prayer 11*.
36. Ibid., Vol. 1., p. 236.
37. Ibid., Vol. 2, pp. 6–7. From *The Church Porch*.
38. Walton, op. cit., p. 65.
39. Herbert, op. cit., Vol. 2, p. 178.
40. Ibid., p. 218.
41. Walton, op. cit., p. 68.
42. Herbert, op. cit., Vol, 1. p. 207.
43. Ibid., Vol. 2, pp. 15–16. From *The Church Porch*.
44. Walton, op. cit., p. 73.
45. Herbert, op. cit., Vol. 2, p. 200. From *Aaron*.

46. Ibid., pp. 119–20. *The British Church.*

47. Ibid., p. 65. From *Church-Music.*

48. Walton, op. cit., p. 74.

49. Herbert, op. cit., Vol. 2, p. 65. From *Church-Music.*

50. Ibid., p. 146. From *Man's Medley.*

51. Ibid., pp. 130–1, 133. From *Providence.*

52. Walton, op. cit., pp. 90–1.

53. Herbert's words were, 'If he can think it may turn to the advantage of any . . . dejected poor soul, let it be made public, if not let him burn it, for I and it are less than the least of God's mercies.' Ibid., p. 90.

54. Ibid.

55. Herbert, op. cit., Vol. 2, p. 179. From *Praise iii.*

56. Ibid., p. 189. From *The Flower.*

57. Ibid., p. 66.

58. J. Donne, *Devotions by John Donne, D. D., Dean of St. Paul's with Two Sermons: I. On the Decease of Lady Danvers, mother of George Herbert; II. Death's Duel – His Own Funeral* (London, 1840), pp. 188, 194–5.

59. Ibid., p. 188.

60. Ibid., pp. 190, 195–6.

61. Herbert, op. cit., Vol. 2, p. 11. From *The Church Porch.*

62. Walton, op. cit., pp. 89–90.

63. Blackstone, op. cit., p. 58.

64. Walton, op. cit., pp. 92–3.

65. Ibid., pp. 92, 94–6.

66. His mother was a close friend of John Donne who dedicated his poem *The Autumnal* to her:
    No Spring, nor Summer Beauty has such grace,
    As I have seen in one Autumnal face.

67. Herbert, op. cit., Vol. 2, pp. 52–3. From *The Temper.*

68. Ibid., pp. 50–1. *Antiphon.*

69. Ibid., pp. 165–6. *Praise ii.*

70. Ibid., p. 60. From *Praise i.*

71. Ibid., pp. 15–17. From *The Church Porch.*

72. Ibid., p. 166. From *An Offering.*

73. Ibid., p. 48. From *Prayer i.*

74. Ibid., pp. 82–3. From *Denial.*

75. Ibid., p. 18. From *The Church Porch.*

76. F. E. Hutchinson, ed. *The Works of George Herbert* (Oxford, 1945), p. 203. *Evensong*.
77. Herbert, op. cit., Vol. 2, pp. 206–7. From *The Invitation*.
78. Ibid., pp. 208–10. *The Banquet*.
79. This is a theory of the Eucharist which asserts Christ's local presence after the Consecration.
80. Hutchinson, op. cit., pp. 200–1. *The H. Communion*.
81. Herbert, op. cit., Vol. 2, pp. 48–50, *Holy Communion*.
82. Ibid., p. 19. *The Altar*.
83. Ibid., pp. 217–18. *Love iii*.
84. Ibid., pp. 92–3. *Virtue*.
85. Ibid., p. 80. From *To all Angels and Saints*.
86. Ibid., pp. 189–90. From *The Flower*.
87. Ibid., pp. 163–4. From *The Discharge*.
88. Ibid., p. 216. *Judgment*.
89. Ibid., pp. 213–14. From *Death*.
90. Ibid., pp. 216–7. *Heaven*.
91. Ibid., p. 84. *Christmas*.
92. Ibid., pp. 84–5.*Christmas*.
93. Ibid., p. 55, From *Jordan*.
94. Ibid., p. 91–2. *Lent*.
95. Ibid., pp., 40–1. *Nature*.
96. Ibid., p. 86. From *Ungratefulness*.
97. Ibid., p. 141. From *Confession*.
98. Ibid., p. 109. From *Misery*.
99. Ibid., pp. 49–50. From *Holy Communion*.
100. Ibid., pp. 86–7. *Sighs and Groans*.
101. Ibid., pp. 107–8. From *Misery*.
102. Ibid., p. 66. *Church-lock and Key*.
103. Ibid., p. 135. *Sins Round*.
104. Ibid., pp. 44–5. *Repentance*.
105. Ibid., pp. 20–9. *The Sacrifice*.
106. Ibid., p. 33. *Good Friday*.
107. Ibid., pp. 34–5. *Redemption*.
108. Ibid., pp. 187–8. *The Cross*.
109. Ibid., pp. 195–6. *Self Condemnation*.
110. Ibid., p. 179. From *Clasping of Hands*.
111. Ibid., pp. 36–7. *Easter*.
112. Ibid., p. 38. *Easter Wings*.

113. Ibid., p. 122. *The Dawning.*
114. Ibid., pp. 197–8.*The 23rd Psalm.*
115. Ibid., pp. 58–9. *Whitsunday.*
116. Ibid., pp. 59–60. *Grace.*
117. Ibid., p. 68. *Trinity Sunday.*
118. Ibid., pp. 198–9. *Marie Magdalen.*
119. Ibid., pp. 80–1. *To All Angels and Saints.*
120. Ibid., p. 123. *Jesu.*
121. Ibid., p. 52. *Love 11.*
122. Ibid., p. 4. From *The Church Porch.*
123. Ibid., pp. 137–8. *Gratefulness.*
124. Ibid., p. 7. From *The Church Porch.*
125. Ibid., pp. 9, 12–13. From *The Church Porch.*
126. Ibid., pp. 13–14. From *The Church Porch.*
127. Ibid., p. 15. From *The Church Porch.*
128. Ibid., p. 13. From *The Church Porch.*
129. Ibid., pp. 73–4. *Constancy.*
130. Ibid., pp. 1–2. From *The Church Porch.*
131. Ibid., p. 4. From *The Church Porch.*
132. Ibid., p. 7. From *The Church Porch.*
133. Ibid., p. 11. From *The Church Porch.*
134. Ibid., p. 3. From *The Church Porch.*
135. Ibid., pp. 2–3. From *The Church Porch.*
136. Ibid., p. 10. From *The Church Porch*, no. 41.
137. Ibid., p. 6. From *The Church Porch.*
138. Ibid., p. 212. From *The Elixir.*

Bibliography

BLACKSTONE, B. Ed. *The Ferrar Papers* (Cambridge, 1938).

DONNE, J. *Devotions by John Donne DD, Dean of St. Paul's with Two Sermons: I. On the Decease of Lady Danvers, Mother of George Herbert, and II. Death's Duel – His Own Funeral Sermon* (London, 1840).

HERBERT, G. *The Works of George Herbert in Prose and Verse*, 2 vols. (London, 1859).

HUTCHINSON, F. E. *The Works of George Herbert* (Clarendon Press, Oxford, 1941).